YOUR KNOWLEDGE HAS VALUE

Bibliographic information published by the German National Library:

The German National Library lists this publication in the National Bibliography; detailed bibliographic data are available on the Internet at http://dnb.dnb.de .

Imprint:

Copyright © 2016 GRIN Verlag, Open Publishing GmbH
Print and binding: Books on Demand GmbH, Norderstedt Germany
ISBN: 9783668261730

This book at GRIN:

http://www.grin.com/en/e-book/336322/exchange-programs-the-effects-on-a-young-person-concerning-cognitive-and

Viktoria Schneeweiß

Aus der Reihe: e-fellows.net stipendiaten-wissen

e-fellows.net (Hrsg.)

Band 2014

Exchange programs. The effects on a young person concerning cognitive and emotional skills

GRIN Publishing

GRIN - Your knowledge has value

Since its foundation in 1998, GRIN has specialized in publishing academic texts by students, college teachers and other academics as e-book and printed book. The website www.grin.com is an ideal platform for presenting term papers, final papers, scientific essays, dissertations and specialist books.

Visit us on the internet:

http://www.grin.com/

http://www.facebook.com/grincom

http://www.twitter.com/grin_com

Effects of an exchange programme on a young person concerning cognitive and emotional skills

Vorwissenschaftliche Arbeit verfasst von

Februar 2016

BRG/BORG St.Pölten

Abstract

More and more young people decide to spend a few months of their school time in a foreign country. This paper deals with the effects of an exchange programme and reveals possible consequences on a cognitive basis as well as ones on a personal basis.

I have decided to write about that topic because during my upper classes I took part in an exchange programme and wanted to find out whether my experience denotes a 'usual' stay and its consequences.

Although there are great effects on young people's knowledge, an exchange influences them personally a lot more than cognitive. Gaining self-confidence, maturity and openness towards new situations and other cultures are only a little selection of what former exchange students reported to have experienced.

The findings are based on a survey with a total of 132 respondents, 98 of them being former exchange students and 34 being in the planning phase of their adventure. The results coincided with the considered previous studies on the same issue by and large, although some significant differences like the number of students spending their time in the USA compared to the ones who spend their exchange elsewhere occurred.

Table of contents

1. Introduction and lead-in to the procedure of an exchange programme based on the programmes of "into Schüleraustausch"

1.1. Introduction

> *„Der institutionelle internationale Austausch, der Jugendliche zum Reisen bringt, zum Aufenthalt in einem anderen Land und zu dessen Entdeckung, zum Erleben von Begegnungssituationen mit dessen Einwohnern, erscheint als eine natürliche und angemessene Antwort für die Zielsetzung einer Annäherung der Kulturen, der Kenntnis des Anderen und der Kommunikation mit ihm."* [1] *(Colin, 2006, p. 281)*

What Lucette Colin wrote in 2006 exhibits only one facet of student's exchange. Apart from being a means of getting different cultures together, it is also a way to learn a second language up to native speaker level and it also illustrates a great possibility for young people to unfold themselves, to expand their horizon and to dispute with themselves.

I took part in an exchange programme myself in 2014 and therefore wanted to investigate the effects of such a stay in general. Two of my central questions were "Can it be said generally that an exchange student, seen personally and characterwise, ages twice as fast during their time abroad?" and "Does my own experience reflect a 'usual' exchange and its consequences?".

The following pages will deal with the issue of how taking part in an exchange programme affects a young person. Of course, beside cognitive effects there are a lot

---

[1] The institutional international exchange that gets adolescents to travelling, to a stay in a foreign country and to its discovery, to the experience of encounter situations with its inhabitants seems to be a natural and appropriate answer for the ambition of an approach of cultures, the acquaintance of the other one and the communication with them.

of changes in personality that a long time abroad at such a young age will cause. This paper will reveal what kind of changes most exchange students face with themselves and find out whether a kind of paragon of how an exchange student diversifies exists or not.

In order to receive reliable answers, the questionnaire which provides the basis for this disquisition consulted 98 returnees [2] and 34 hopees [3] of "into Schüleraustausch". It contained detailed questions concerning expectations on how the exchange will change the young people and their delivery.

1.2. The time before the exchange – being a "HOPEE"

In order to become an exchange student with "into Schüleraustausch" one has to apply at least three months before the actual beginning of the programme (into GmbH, 2014, p. 38). The first step is the pre-application, which can be filled in online or sent in manually. After that, the hopee has to pass through an interview with one of "into Schüleraustausch's" employees. The organisation then decides whether or not a person is suitable for an exchange. After being chosen the student gets a link to the so called "application forms", twelve pages where detailed information about the student and their life is required. These forms must be sent to "into" within four weeks. Apart from that the hopee and their parents have to sign a comprehensive contract with "into Schüleraustausch". The organisation signs that contract back after having received all of the required forms (into GmbH, 2014, p. 4).

Once everything is filled in and sent, the waiting time starts. The date of receiving the placement is independent from the time of application. Therefore "into" is able to find the most appropriate host family for everyone (into GmbH, 2014, p. 5). During or after the waiting time (depends on the time of getting a placement) "into"

---

[2] Former exchange students
[3] Students who have already planned, but not yet started their exchange programme

offers an obligatory pre-departure-seminar (PDS) with all hopees and several re-turnees. On the same weekend they also offer an information evening for all parents, which is not compulsory, but advisable (into GmbH, 2014, p. 5).

1.3. Different types of exchange programmes

The term "exchange programme" denotes a certain time which is spent abroad by a student, it can roughly be separated into short- and long-time exchange. This paper is only going to deal with long-time exchange, which means a single student spends at least one month in a foreign country, usually when they are between fourteen and eighteen years old (Thomas, 1988, p. 290). The actual duration of that time can vary, the range of offered programmes includes one-month-stays as well as twenty-months-stays. According to "into Schüleraustausch"[4] the most common programmes are half a school year or one school year abroad.

In Austria, any student who has stayed in a foreign country between five and twelve months and successfully completed the school year there is automatically allowed to graduate into the next class (SchUG, 01.07.2015, § 25 (9)). However, "into Schüleraustausch" guarantees the recognition of any of their programmes, also the shorter ones, and therefore offers their students security (into GmbH, 2014, p. 4).

Apart from their duration, exchange programmes can be distinguished by the type of payment. For the nowadays more popular type the exchange student has to pay a certain amount of money to the exchange organisation which will cover any costs like school fees or the money for the host family. The other possibility is taking someone from the host country as an exchange student after or before the own exchange and therefore pay less. This paper is only going to deal with the more favoured type of exchange programmes.

---

[4] I took part in one of "into Schüleraustausch's" exchange programmes. The organisation contracted into supporting me with my "VWA".

As mentioned above, taking part in an exchange programme costs money. The price range reaches from about 5.000€ up to a lot more than 20.000€ depending on the country and duration of the stay (into GmbH, 2014, pp. 25, 35). Some organisations offer scholarships for very few students. "into Schüleraustausch" only offers these for their "USA CLASSIC" programme and the decision whether or not the financial situation of a student really requires support is in the hands of their tax accountant. There are also several other institutions to get financial backup, for example the Austrian Federal Ministry of Education and Culture or the so called "Michael von Zoller"-foundation (Arreola, 2016; http://www.into.at/schueleraustausch/links.html, 2016-02-03).

1.4. The time of the exchange – being an "EXCHANGE STUDENT"

After their arrival most[5] exchange students who leave their home country in summer take part in an orientation camp which lasts between four and eight days. It takes place in a central city of the host country and the caretakers show the students around. In Spain "into" also offers language-workshops to ease the exchange students' access into living with Spanish-speaking people. After that everyone gets to their host family, where the real exchange starts (into GmbH, 2014, p. 8f).

Every area with exchange students has a so called "Local Rep."[6] who helps out in case any problems occur and makes sure the students as well as the host families are alright and satisfied with each other. Apart from that "into" offers a 24/7-emergency-hotline for very urgent problems (into GmbH, 2014, p. 7). In order to solve any problem properly, the organisation has an emergency chain which starts with talking to the host family, goes on with contacting the Local Rep., getting in

---

[5] Orientation camps are only offered for certain countries, so not all students have the possibility to take part in such a camp.
[6] Short form of "Local Representative"

touch with the organisations[7] and ends with calling the parents at home (into Schüleraustausch GmbH, 2013, p. 9).

If serious issues between host family and exchange student emerge, "into" offers the possibility of changing host family, together with their partner organisation they will then try to find a more appropriate host family very soon (into GmbH, 2014, p. 7). However, they always want their exchange students to at least try to get on with their new surroundings for a few weeks before they can change host family.

1.5. The time after the exchange – being a "RETURNEE"

It is entirely up to the exchange student, who is now a "returnee", to decide whether they want to keep in touch with "into" or just see their exchange as checked and not have any more contact with the organisation. "into Schüleraustausch" offers a returnee-seminar for all returnees every year. Moreover, they have a so called "returnee-point-system". Former exchange students can do different activities like helping at a pre-departure-seminar or informing other people about "into" in order to gain returnee-points. After having earned enough points (a flight inside Europe for example "costs" around 1.000 returnee-points) "into" agrees to pay for a flight back to the host country. That way they enable a lot of returnees to meet their host families again and keep in touch with them (into GmbH, 2014, p. 5).

Returnees also get the possibility to give feedback on their exchange to "into", so the organisation can always improve their programmes. Very frequently, they are told that certain Local Reps do not supervise the students well enough. The organisation of course tries to improve in that point, but they also mentioned that the job

---

[7] They suggest contacting their partner organisation in the host country first and the Austrian one afterwards.

of a local coordinator is to find a proper host family for any student and not to organise a lot of trips and excursions. However, most returnees give positive feedback to "into", for instance they tell them that they had the best time of their life or feel a lot more independent after their stay abroad. What is more, many exchange students who have just come home from their journey say to be much more aware of their own culture (Arreola, 2016).

Any former exchange student is a returnee for the rest of their life. So to speak, all effects that are due to taking part in such an exchange programme and that will show up at some point in one's life will be apparent with a returnee. Therefore, the following chapter deals with the effects of an exchange according to previous studies.

2. Effects of an exchange according to previous studies

Student's exchange is an issue which has only predominantly been researched in final papers as yet (Thomas, 1988, p. 289; Hürter, 2008, p. 15). Therefore hardly any long-term studies are in existence, which is why some aspects are always ignored and the results often do not coincide (Hürter, 2008, p. 22). Moreover, the majority of studies into that topic deals with exchange during the time at university, but as it has been found out that the age of an exchange student matters only subordinately, such papers and studies are also going to be taken into consideration (Richter-Trummer, 2002, p. 114f).

2.1. General information on country of chosen exchange programmes as well as age and gender of exchange students

In a research with over 1000 former exchange students who had gone abroad with YFU[8] between 1998 and 2005 about 65% of the exchange students were female. More than three quarters of those respondents chose the United States of America as their exchange destination. A quite big difference between female and male students could be noticed in that case: With the girls more than one quarter decided to go to another country than the USA, whereas only 14% of the boys did so (Hürter, 2008, p. 82).

The margin of exchange student's age was from 15 to 18 years in that study. Again, there was a significant distinction concerning gender. The girls were generally younger than the boys when they started their exchange programme. What is

---

[8] Short form for the exchange-organisation "Youth For Understanding" (http://www.yfu.at/impressum, 2016-01-10)

more, while more than 90% of the USA-students went abroad after their tenth year of school, nearly 20% of the others started it either after their ninth or eleventh year (Hürter, 2008, p. 83).[9]

2.2. School after an exchange

Only less than a quarter of the YFU-students repeated the missed school year, therefore a difference between repeaters and non-repeaters occurred. While nearly 24% of the non-repeaters faced troubles at school back home, only 17% of the repeaters did so. Apart from that, female returnees had a lot more problems at school after their exchange than their male colleagues and exchange students who had gone to another country than the USA were more likely to have a hard time catching up than the ones who had stayed somewhere in the United States of America (Hürter, 2008, p. 91).

In general, only about one quarter of the questioned returnees had worse marks after taking part in an exchange programme, about one fifth levelled off and more than half of the students were even able to achieve better marks than they had before their time in a foreign country (Hürter, 2008, p. 106).

When looking at the grades in specific subjects before and after the exchange Hürter (2008, pp. 95, 99) found out that about half of the exchange students stayed the same in Maths and German, while one quarter was able to improve their marks and one quarter's marks deteriorated after their time abroad. Unsurprisingly, this was very different with the first foreign language[10], there only about 5% recorded a worse mark after their exchange (this might be due to the fact that not all students stayed in a country with their first language as mother tongue and furthermore did

---

[9] In contrast to Austrian students, in Germany all students who are doing their A-levels have 13 years of school, therefore the time span for going abroad is longer than with the 12-year-system in Austria.
[10] In 90% of the cases this was English, the other 10% had Latin, French, Spanish or Russian as their first foreign language.

not have the opportunity to attend lessons for that language), 35% remained constant and nearly 60% could enhance their performance (Hürter, 2008, p. 103).

The general improvement in school subjects in contempt of the missed subject matter was amongst other things reasoned with better language knowledge, higher self-confidence and a more conscious approach to school. A high number of returnees agreed that they learnt to realise their own aims and to assess themselves more easily because of the exchange. Additionally, more than two thirds said they were better able to organise themselves and nearly half of the questionees registered higher motivation for attending school after coming back home (Hürter, 2008, p. 110f).

Similar results were found with exchange during university-time, but although the integration of taken exams in the foreign country can constitute a problem in some cases and missed courses etc. might extend the duration of study an exchange cannot be called a wasted year of study. A lot of exchange students gained experience in other parts of life that turned out to be helpful in their studies some time later (Richter-Trummer, 2002, p. 117).

2.3. Effects on the future career

As per Hürter's study on a scale from zero ("The exchange had no impact on my career choice.") to five ("The exchange had a great impact on my career choice.") the midpoint was at 3.22, so obviously the impact is quite high. Only 2% of the included former exchange students claimed that their time abroad had no influence on their career possibilities at all, which shows quite clearly that in general it can be said that taking part in an exchange programme will most certainly take an impact on one's future career. Even though, hardly any students were motivated to go on exchange by the prospect of having better chances at the employment market (Hürter, 2008, p. 111ff).

With another study called "Erlebnisse, die verändern"[11] 17% of all returnees who had taken part in long-time exchange programmes said their time abroad had no effect on the choice of career, whereas a significantly higher number of students who had only taken part in short-time programmes agreed with that statement. This supports the thesis that the longer the stay lasts, the more distinctive the repercussions are (Hürter, 2008, p. 114). Separate trial found out that 75% of exchange students change their future perspectives during their stay abroad (Richter-Trummer, 2002, p. 111).

2.4. Effects on personal skills

Although an exchange does not affect the assessment of the importance of development tasks[12] it influences their coping. In a study with 100 university students without an exchange and 71 students with some study time abroad, it turned out that no matter what age the exchange students were, they had a higher overall level of accomplishment of development tasks after their exchange. There had been two inquiries with both groups, one at the beginning of their degree course and one in the year when the paper was published, when they had already worked at least part of their way through their studies. In the first survey, the non-exchange students estimated themselves a little higher in having coped their development tasks than the exchange students did. The second interrogation showed that during their exchange, the abroad students "overtook" their colleagues in accomplishing their developmental targets, which shows that a longer stay abroad during study time can express a way of influencing the own personal progress (Richter-Trummer, 2002, p. 107f).

Especially the areas "peer"[13], "detachment"[14] and "self"[15] showed a faster progress with the exchange students. Being abroad alone and building up a "new" life for a

---

[11] Experiences that change
[12] 10 development tasks listed by Dreher & Dreher in 1985 (Scheid, 2002, p. 104)
[13] Structure of a circle of friends

limited time requires self-confidence and self-consciousness and enables inde-pendence, which connotes detachment from the parental home. Getting to know people in the foreign country and establishing a group of friends necessitates active approach and communication, wherefore the young people make a faster advance in accomplishing the task "peer". What is more, in contrast to being at home, where someone will always know you, in another country you can reinvent yourself. This of course takes the ability to have a showdown with yourself and get to know who you are, respectively who you want to be. Due to that, exchange stu-dents tend to cope the target "self" quicker than non-exchange students do (Richter-Trummer, 2002, p. 108f).

Moreover, shifting for oneself at such a young age makes people a lot more distinct and therefore changes them. In Richter-Trummer's survey 86% of exchange stu-dents said their personality changed at least moderately during their time abroad. These people also seem to become more open towards changes as well as other cultures, which once might play an important role in the fight against xenophobia as someone who has once experienced what being a stranger means will act differ-ently towards strangers in their own country (Richter-Trummer, 2002, p. 113).

Another skill that will most certainly be improved by an exchange is the ability of assimilating oneself into new situations and organising one's everyday life in a dif-ferent way. This will make it easier to get on with unknown problems that may oc-cur in further life (Richter-Trummer, 2002, p. 113). Another study found out that most exchange students agree to be better able to handle conflict situations than they were before their time abroad (Hürter, 2008, p. 127).

---

[14] Detaching from the parents
[15] Knowing who you are and what you want

[14]

2.5. Intercultural learning as an aspect of exchange programmes

Although only few exchange students really gain enduring knowledge on intercultural aspects, most of them at least manage to *"relativise"* their own culture. Intercultural learning means to shed prejudice by living with people of the prejudged civilization and calling certain behaviour that others might call childish or *"unbearable"* just English or French or Spanish. A journey that includes attending an educational institution abroad can contribute a lot more to a young person's intercultural learning than for example a private voyage to a foreign country (Colin, 2006, p. 282f).

However, an observational study found out that in most cases only step one of intercultural learning, "amplification of cognizance about the foreign culture", could be reached. Only some instances showed an attainment of step two, "cognition of the partners' mental structure" (Denne, 1988, p. 302).

Nevertheless, it cannot be predicted in what way and quality intercultural learning will be part of an exchange in advance as firstly it depends on its explicit and the tacit aims and secondly responsible teachers and their educational competence to stimulate processes of intercultural learning also figure prominently (Thomas, 1988, p. 292).

2.6. Language skills

Exchange includes learning a language by immersion. That means the language is not taught as a single subject at school, but any subject is taught in that tongue. It is so to speak used as the working language (Larcher, 2012, p. 71). In addition to that, exchange students obviously also get to improve their language skills by talking to people – a supplement to the scholar language study. Therefore, exchange programmes are the best way to help our modern society get bilingual people who represent part of the new elite (Colin, 2006, p. 281).

Moreover, an exchange does not only help to improve one single language, it also motivates young people to learn further foreign languages. This is most certainly attributable to the lower inhibition threshold towards communicating in other languages that is caused by an exchange. However, this mostly applies to long-time programmes, a two-week-stay during summer holidays will not seriously change the attitude and motivation towards learning new languages (Hürter, 2008, p. 114f).

As I have done research on that topic myself, the following chapter will examine the results of my questionnaires and find out whether or not they concur with what the mentioned studies and papers reported about student's exchange.

3. Effects of an exchange according to my own research

3.1. General information on chosen programmes

The results of the research showed that nearly 90% of students going abroad are female. This came quite unexpected because when I was on exchange in Callan myself, I had the impression that the number of female and male exchangers was approximately the same.

However, the average age of 15.77 years at the time the exchange starts verifies what "into Schüleraustausch" told me. Due to the Austrian school system, which suggests going abroad either during the tenth grade (at a school with four years of senior classes) or the eleventh grade (at a school with five years of senior classes), most exchange students from here are still quite young when they start their adventure.

The choice of destination amongst "into"-students is quite diverse, as they go to 14 different countries (with the USA counted as 1 country). Although there is such a wide range of different nations they can go to, more than half of the students spend their exchange somewhere in the USA. This coincides with previous studies, compared to some, the number of USA-students is actually on the bottom line of what was to be expected (Hürter, 2008, p. 82). The second most preferred country is the United Kingdom, but the gap between these two nations is huge – only 15% decide to go to Great Britain. Only one more country is visited by a binary percentage of exchange students, 12% of them take their time in Canada. The left 20% of "into Schüleraustausch's" exchange students branch out more or less equally on the following countries:

- Australia
- Costa Rica

- France
- Ireland
- Italy
- New Zealand
- Norway
- South Africa
- Spain
- Sweden
- The Netherlands

Amongst those countries, Ireland and France are the frontrunners, with 6% respectively 4% of the exchange students going there.

FRANCE	4%
IRELAND	6%
CANADA	9%
OTHERS	13%
UK	14%
USA	54%

Although "into Schüleraustausch" offers a variety of possible durations of exchange programmes (1 month, 2 months, 3 months, 5 months, 6 months, 8 months, 10 months, 11 months, 2 years) (into GmbH, 2014, p. 11ff), 94% of their students either go abroad for five or for ten months (46% choose the shorter programme and 48% go for the longer version). Amongst the questioned students there was no one who had gone/was going abroad for two years, which might be attributable to the fact that "into" has only offered these extra-long programmes for a short time (Arreola, 2016). Moreover, the shortest chosen option was five months; this is probably due to the Austrian law that says that an exchange is only fully recognised with a minimum duration of five months (SchUG, 01.07.2015, § 25 (9)). Another occurrence that can most certainly be traced back to our law is that not even 8% of those who go abroad repeat the missed school year at their Austrian school. That stands in contradistinction to German exchange students, because of the different school system about one quarter of those repeat the missed school year (Hürter, 2008, p. 89).

3.2. Effects on the future life

Even though most students just skip an enormous part of a school year, only 26% of the returnees said they actually had trouble keeping up with their Austrian class-mates after the exchange. This shows quite well that an exchange does not mean becoming worse at school or missing a lot, seen from the educational point of view. When I think of myself, I have to say that not only I learnt quite a lot of useful things for my Austrian classes in Ireland, but it was also fairly easy to make up for the missed subject matter beside my usual scholar duties. This might be because I had to study considerably less for subjects like English after the exchange and therefore had more time for others such as Maths.

That leads to the next point – the language skills exchange students are able to gain during their time abroad. 99% of all respondents strongly agreed or agreed with the statement "My English (or any other language, depending on the host country) im-proved a lot"; furthermore 85% of those at least intend to work internationally be-cause of their improved language abilities. That shows how important exchange is for getting international people at the labour market in the future. If a young per-son has the possibility to explore life elsewhere for a certain time, they get an ex-pansive horizon and very often lose the fear of being away from their usual life and the surroundings they know.

Trying to support their returnees with staying internationally connected, "into Schüleraustausch" offers them to gain so called "into-points". Any returnee can collect points by:

Activity	"Payment"
Helping in office activities	20 points per hour
Working on the Newslink paper[16]	20 points per hour
Publishing an article about the exchange	100 points
Attending an into-info-event	100 points
Doing a presentation (e.g. at school)	100 points
Sending new students to "into"	200 points
Assisting at a pre-departure-seminar	400 points

These after-exchange-activities also affect a returnee's further life as for example assisting at a PDS[17] gives the possibility to dip into the life of holding seminars. "into's" employees are also present at these workshops and for example give advice on how to present certain things in a comprehensible and clear manner. By attending info-events like exchange fairs former exchange students get the opportunity to sell something to strangers. They have the assignment to enlist as many new exchange students as possible and with the help of "into's" staff, they can learn a lot on good selling techniques. Obviously, tasks like publishing an article about the exchange support writing skills that might come in useful in a later job. As a consequence, doing returnee-activities demonstrates a double benefit for these young people.

Moreover, if a former exchange student has a new idea for spreading information about "into", they often offer points for that as well. After finally having gained enough points, the organisation pays for a flight back to the host country. Even though the points seem quite easy to gain, only 6% of the questioned returnees

---

[16] The Newslink paper is an offer for hopees, they receive it three times before their exchange starts and it contains useful information about language, law, school, culture and more.
[17] Short form of pre-departure-seminar

have already managed to collect enough "into"-points for a return ticket to their host country. The amount of needed points varies by the country you want to go back to:

Country	Needed points
Countries within Europe	Ca. 900 points
USA	Ca. 2400 points
Canada	Ca. 2800 points
South America or South Africa	Ca. 2800 points
Australia	Ca. 3700 points
New Zealand	Ca. 3900 points

Interestingly enough, although 80% said they wanted to go back to their host country only a little more than 20% of "into's" returnees have actually gained any points yet. That leads to the inference that many organise and pay for their return to the host country by themselves. I have gained 850 points so far and as I am certain of being able to get another 50 points during the next few months, I will hopefully be visiting my Irish hosts next summer. I also intend to work in Ireland for a few weeks then, which is again going to offer me new international connections.

For some students, their exchange did not only affect their knowledge and perception, but it also helped them choose what to do in their future. A total of 38% were helped to choose their career by the exchange. Even though they might have had a plan in head before, 44% of the exchange students changed that caused at least partly by their time abroad. Most of these people decided to take a gap year[18] instead of pulling their study or working plans straight through.

What is more, about 95% of all former exchange students started studying at a college or university at some point after getting their leaving certificates (some

---

[18] Taking a gap year means doing something else than studying between school and usually university (alternatively working) for one year. Very often gap years are used for doing travel & work or joining social projects.

respondents were in their last year of school when they answered their survey and just revealed their future plans, though they were included in that result) . Therefore, it can be said that the vast majority of exchange students is once going to be working as white-collar-workers and an exchange makes a future in a low-paying-job quite improbable. However, what has to be taken into account is that this may also be related to the fact that an exchange costs a lot and the people who can afford it probably put a lot of money in good education as well. As a result, it might not be the exchange itself that makes the students become well-educated people, but their initial situation that allows such a long time in a foreign country in the first place.

3.3. Influence on personality & character

As anticipated, apart from having a huge effect on the cognitive skills of a young person, an exchange of course affects their personality as well (Richter-Trummer, 2002, p. 113). That is proved by the fact that only 2% of the interviewees agreed with the assertion "The exchange didn't affect my personality at all".

However, in contrast to the interference on school performance and career choice, the results in that category are not that clear and obvious. The clearest outcome is that over 90% of the returnees said to be more mature than others at their age, who have not been abroad for such a long time.

The ability of understanding other people's points of view is clearly affected by an exchange as well, 85% of the respondents agreed that they had less trouble with that after their time in a foreign country. As a result of that advantage, more than 60% of the students got on better with their parents after the exchange, although it has to be stated clearly that this applies for the female pollees, within the boys not even a third agreed with the statement "I got on better with my parents after the exchange".

These results match exactly with what most hopees were expecting before having started their exchange programme. Nevertheless, some of the exchange students tend to expect a lot more than actually happens. About 30% of the returnees said their expectations were not met in the end because they had expected too much. Most agreed that in reality they did not change into entirely new personalities, although they had thought so before their exchange. Some respondents wrote things like *"I thought that I would change more"* when they were asked if they felt their expectations concerning how the exchange would affect themselves were actually fulfilled. Nearly 15% even described that their expectations had been so big that they eventually prevented themselves from enjoying their time enough. Some put the blame of not changing a lot on their high expectations concerning that topic. According to that, too high expectations might turn out to have the opposite effect and interfere with the process of personal development and change during the exchange.

The following is a quotation by one of the respondents, which seems to summarize the effect of a student's exchange on the personality of a young individual perfectly:

> *"I am more self-confident, spontaneous and much more open minded. Furthermore my attitude, regarding to unknown future events and the combined anxiety which comes with them changed a lot. I am not as bound to home as I was before my exchange."*

3.4. Language skills

As expected the respondent's language skills improved in nearly all cases. A lot of them had expected their language skills concerning the one spoken in the host country to improve a lot, some even wrote things like *"I expected my English to improve on an academic level"*, but then mentioned that it turned out differently. Most returnees just reported a huge improvement in spoken language as well as in colloquial language, whereas hardly anyone told about huge improvement in written language. This might be due to the fact that requirements especially concerning written English at Austrian schools are quite different to what is needed and used in countries with English as the mother tongue. In my own case, for example, it turned out that my written English was even better than that of most Irish pupils as I had had to learn any grammar and spelling rule by heart at home while they just had a minor focus on these things.

For that reason an exchange is extremely useful for communication in a foreign language – a skill which is needed in almost any job nowadays. However, in contrast to some people's expectations, it does not create brilliant language teachers who are living dictionaries and never make any mistake. That is proved by statements like *"I expected to improve my English skills more."* or *"My English didn't improve on an academic level, I just got better concerning slang and especially South African colloquial speech"*.

3.5. Significant differences between certain groups of exchange students

When looking at the duration of the stay, two large groups can be separated from each other: Exchange students who stayed half a school-year (5-6 months) and exchange students who stayed one school-year (10 months). The first significant difference that occurred is whether the exchange students repeated the missed year or not. 98% of those who stayed only about 5 months "jumped" the year, whereas 10% of the participants of longer programmes repeated. Concerning maturity, in the group whose exchange programmes lasted longer 100% covered an increase in matureness. In contrast to that, only 90% of the ones who stayed half a year agreed with the statement "I was more mature after the exchange (in comparison to others in the same age who hadn't been abroad)".

Another interesting serendipity was made by the comparison of the group of exchange students who spent their time abroad in an English speaking country and those who were in a state with a different mother tongue. Only a bit less than 85% of the students in English speaking destinations intend to work internationally in their future life, whereas 95% of the others do so. Moreover, the English speaking group was more likely to keep their group of friends similar after the exchange than the lot of the other pupils.

A further possible separation is parting the questioned returnees into USA-students and NON-USA-students. Doing that showed that exchange students who had stayed in the United States of America rather faced problems at school in Austria afterwards than the ones who had gone elsewhere did. About two thirds of the USA-students told about troubles whereas only a little more than a fifth of the rest did so. What is more, the very few students who strongly agreed with the statement "I had trouble keeping up with my Austrian classmates at school after the exchange" were all USA-students.

Some significant differences concerning the effects of an exchange programme could be spotted in the comparison of female and male participants. While more than 60% of the male exchange students agreed that their circle of friends changed caused by the time abroad, only less than 40% of the girls said this applied to themselves. A similar course was discovered within the relationship to the students' parents. More than 60% of the female returnees told about an even better relationship to their parents after the exchange, whereas only around 40% of the boys registered that. This is especially interesting as studies have found out that in general the relationship between parents and a daughter and the one between parents and a son do not differ significantly (Roth, 2012, p. 303). Therefore, the contention that boys have a better relationship to their parents in general and as a consequence the same cannot become better is invalidated. When it comes to school, the female respondents noted down a lower probability of having trouble at school after the exchange than the male ones did. Moreover, it turned out that girls are less likely to be helped choose what to do after school by their exchange. Only about 35% of them agreed with the statement „The exchange helped me choose what to do after school", whilst more than 45% of the male exchange students said this was true for them.

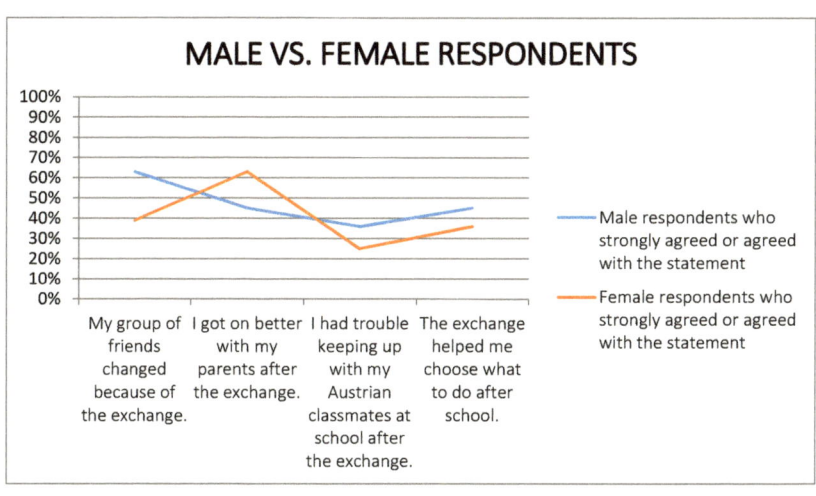

4. Conclusion

There is no longer any doubt that taking part in an exchange programme affects a young person's life. While the research revealed fewer cognitive effects than expected, the consequences on a personal basis turned out to be astonishing.

Although a certain time spent abroad during school years helps improve one's spoken language skills enormously, it does not necessarily enhance the written performance. This is most surely due to the fact that the aspects of a language that are focussed in a country with the same as mother tongue differ significantly from those in focus at a school where the language is taught as a foreign language. Therefore, contrary to quite a few hopees' expectations, an exchange will not leave young people who are able to speak and write English (or any other language, depending on the one spoken in the host country) on an academic level.

In contrast to that, the impact on maturity and self-confidence is huge. Hardly any exchange student would agree not to have been affected by their time abroad concerning these areas. By implication, an exchange leaves young people more mature and more grown-up than their peers who did not take part in an exchange programme and the question whether or not it is true that an exchange student ages faster character-wise during the time abroad can most definitely be answered positively. However, the extent of how much such an exchange can affect a pupil cannot be predicted as it depends very much on the individual student's willingness and motivation towards that experience.

A further issue that has not been taken into consideration at all in the very beginning, but also turned out to be quite important is the aspect of intercultural learning. Not only does it matter for a young person's later life whether or not they have learnt a lot about intercultural facets, but it also matters for our whole companion. A society that consists of open-minded people who can look back on intercultural experiences and who are able to understand other cultures' ways of thinking and acting will work a lot better on a permanent basis than one with people who only know and accept their own civilization. Consequently, exchange programmes denote a lot more than just a certain time that is advantageous for one individual, in reality they also declare an important step forward concerning the peaceful cohabitation of different peoples.

Bibliography

Schulunterrichtsgesetz (SchUG). Gemäß Stand vom 01.07.2015.

Arreola, A. (2016). *Correspondence*. Wien.

Colin, L. (2006). Schüleraustausch und Grenzen der Schule. In H. Nicklas, B. Müller & H. Kordes (Hrsg.), *Interkulturell denken und handeln*. Frankfurt/Main: Campus Verlag GmbH.

Denne, L. (1988). Resultate der Tagung – Folgerungen für die Praxis. In A. Thomas, *Interkulturelles Lernen im Schüleraustausch*. Saarbrücken: Breitenbach Publishers.

Hürter, L. (2008). *„Entfernung schafft Klarheit" Die Auswirkungen eines im Ausland verbrachten Schuljahres auf die schulischen Leistungen und den weiteren Bildungsweg*. Unveröffentlichte Magisterarbeit, Universität Konstanz.

into GmbH. *Nützliche Hinweise für zukünftige* Austauschschüler. Retrieved from http://www.into.at/schueleraustausch/links.html [2016-02-03].

into GmbH (2014). *High School 2015-2016*. Wien.

into Schüleraustausch GmbH (2013). *Vorbereitung Jänner 2014*. Wien.

Larcher, D. (2012). Drei begegnungspädagogische Ansätze im Vergleich. In S. Baur, *Austauschpädagogik und Austauscherfahrung*. Baltmannsweiler: Schneider Verlag Hohengehren.

Richter-Trummer, T. (2002). *Studieren in Europa: Studienbezogene Auslandsaufenthalte und ihr Einfluss auf die Persönlichkeitsentwicklung junger Erwachsener*. Karl-Franzens-Universität, Graz.

Roth, J. (2012). *Eltern-Kind-Beziehung und elterliche Werteinstellungen*. Kempten: AZ Druck- und Datentechnik.

Scheid, D. (2002). *Einflüsse von studienbezogenen Auslandsaufenthalten auf die Persönlichkeitsentwicklung junger Erwachsener*. Karl-Franzens-Universität, Graz.

[29]

Thomas, A. (1988). Interkulturelles Lernen im Schüleraustausch aus der Sicher der Austauschforschung. In A. Thomas, *Interkulturelles Lernen im Schüleraustausch*. Saarbrücken: Breitenbach Publishers.

Youth For Understanding, Verein. *YFU Austria – Interkultureller Austausch*. Retrieved from http://www.yfu.at/impressum [2016-01-10].

Appendix

Questionnaires

HOPEES

Hello!

My name's Viktoria Schneeweiss and I'm currently writing a paper on the effects of an exchange programme for my Matura. Please be so kind and answer the following questions truthfully. If you have any questions don't hesitate to contact me: viktoriaschneeweiss@gmail.com

Thank you so much!

1. Please tick your gender.

○ Female
○ Male

2. How old are you going to be when you leave for you exchange?

○ 15
○ 16
○ 17
○ Other (please specify) [_____]

3. Where are you going for your exchange?

○ Canada
○ Costa Rica
○ France
○ Ireland
○ New Zealand
○ Spain
○ Sweden
○ UK
○ USA
○ Other (please specify) [_____]

4. How long are you going to stay abroad?

○ 5 months
○ 10 months
○ Other (please specify) [   ]

5. Are you going to repeat the missed year at your Austrian school?

○ Yes
○ No

6. Please tick if you strongly agree, agree, disagree or strongly disagree with the following statements.

	Strongly agree	Agree	Disagree	Strongly disagree
I expect myself to be more mature after the exchange.	○	○	○	○
I expect myself to have a different group of friends after the exchange.	○	○	○	○
I expect myself to understand other people's point of view more easily after the exchange.	○	○	○	○
I don't expect the exchange to affect my personality at all.	○	○	○	○
I'm afraid I will have trouble keeping up with my Austrian classmates at school after my exchange.	○	○	○	○
I expect myself to get on better with my parents after the exchange.	○	○	○	○
I expect myself to know better what I want to do when having finished school after the exchange.	○	○	○	○
I expect myself to go back to my host country a few years after the exchange (for a longer time).	○	○	○	○
I expect my English (or any other language, depending on the host country) to improve a lot.	○	○	○	○
I would like to work internationally once because I think my language skills will be positively affected by the exchange a lot.	○	○	○	○

7. Are there any other expectations you have concerning how your exchange will affect yourself? If yes, please specify.

[   ]

8. What would you like to do after having finished school? (For boys after having completed military or community service)

◯ Take a year off
◯ Go to university
◯ Start working immediately
◯ Other (please specify) [_____]

9. Are you planning to do some work for "into Schüleraustausch" after your stay in order to gain points for a flight back to your hostcountry?

◯ Yes
◯ No

RETURNEES

Hello!

My name's Viktoria Schneeweiss and I'm currently writing a paper on the effects of an exchange programme for my Matura. Please be so kind and answer the following questions truthfully. If you have any questions don't hesitate to contact me: viktoriaschneeweiss@gmail.com

Thank you so much!

1. Please tick your gender.

◯ Female
◯ Male

2. How old are you?

[   ]

3. How old were you when you left for your exchange?

◯ 15
◯ 16
◯ 17
◯ Other (please specify) [_____]

4. Where did you go for your exchange?

- ○ Canada
- ○ Costa Rica
- ○ France
- ○ Ireland
- ○ New Zealand
- ○ Spain
- ○ Sweden
- ○ UK
- ○ USA
- ○ Other (please specify) [   ]

7. Please tick if you strongly agree, agree, disagree or strongly disagree with the following statements.

	Strongly agree	Agree	Disagree	Strongly disagree
I was more mature after the exchange (in comparison to others in the same age who hadn't been abroad).	○	○	○	○
My group of friends changed because of the exchange.	○	○	○	○
I was able to understand other people's point of view more easily after the exchange.	○	○	○	○
The exchange didn't affect my personality at all.	○	○	○	○
I had trouble keeping up with my Austrian classmates at school after the exchange.	○	○	○	○
I got on better with my parents after the exchange.	○	○	○	○
The exchange helped me choose what to do after school.	○	○	○	○
My English (or any other language, depending on the host country) improved a lot.	○	○	○	○
I (intend to) work internationally because the exchange improved my language skills so much that I am now easily able to do so.	○	○	○	○

8. Did you go back to your host country after the exchange for a longer time or are you planning to do so?

- ○ Yes
- ○ No

9. Have you gained any "into-points" for a flight back to your host country yet?

○ Yes
○ No

10. Have you actually managed to gain enough points for a flight mack to your host country?

○ Yes
○ No

11. Do you feel your expectations concerning how the exchange would affect yourself were actually fulfilled?

○ Yes
○ No

12. Why do you feel so?

```


```

13. Did the exchange make you change your future plans?

○ Yes
○ No

14. What are you now doing? (If you're still at school, please choose what you're planning to do after having finished school/military or community service.)

○ Studying at university/college
○ Working (after having finished university/college)
○ Working (I didn't attend any university/college)
○ Other (please specify) [   ]

Correspondence

E-Mails im Original übernommen, Schreibweise sic.

Absender: viktoriaschneeweiss@gmail.com

Empfänger: austria@into-exchange.com

Datum: 28.01.2016

Hallo!

Seit wann bietet ihr denn an für 2 Jahre ins Ausland zu gehen?

Danke und schönen Tag,

Viki

Absender: austria@into-exchange.com

Empfänger: viktoriaschneeweiss@gmail.com

Datum: 01.02.2016

Halllo Viki,

das ist nur für England, und bist jetzt hat nur eine Person das Programm gemacht. Das machen wir seit letztes Jahr!

LG,

Ashley E. Arreola, Eu.MA.sca

into Schüleraustausch GmbH

Währinger Str. 145/15

1180 Wien

fon: +43 1 4787515

fax: +43 1 4786603

austria@into-exchange.com

www.into.at

www.facebook.com/into.at

Absender: viktoriaschneeweiss@gmail.com

Empfänger: austria@into-exchange.com

Datum: 27.01.2016

Hallo Johanna, hallo Ashley,

hier wie besprochen die Fragen:

into bietet (zumindest in der Broschüre) keine Stipendien o.ä. an – gibt es dafür einen bestimmten Grund?

Ihr bekommt ja von allen Returnees Feedback – was sind denn da die häufigsten Kritikpunkte bzw. die positivsten Sachen die genannt werden?

Vielen Dank und ganz liebe Grüße,

Viki

Absender: austria@into-exchange.com

Empfänger: viktoriaschneeweiss@gmail.com

[37]

Datum: 03.02.2016

Hallo Viki,

Wir bieten schon Teilstipendien für das USA CLASSIC Progamm an. Die Entscheidung liegt bei unsere Steuerberaterin und wird auf finanziellen Gebrauch entschieden wieviel, wenn überhaupt ein Schüler etwas bekommt.

Auf unsere Webseite haben wir auch viele verschiedene Quellen genannt, wo man zusätzliche Unterstützung bekommen könnte: http://www.into.at/schueleraustausch/links.html

Kritikpunkte: oft missverstehen die Schüler was sie von ihrem Local Rep erwarten können. Viele meinen, dass der Local Rep zu wenig mit ihnen unternommen hat, zu wenige Aktivitäten organisiert hat oder nicht sehr oft von ihnen gehört. Allerdings ist der Local Rep hauptsächlich da um zu sichern, dass der Schüler gut geht und alles mit der Gastfamilie und Gastschule passt. Sie sind keine Freizeit Aktivitäten Planner, und sie melden sich nur 1x/Monat wenn alles gut läuft. Wenn alles in Ordnung ist, wird man vom Local Rep nicht mitbekommen, da er/sie schon eine gute Dienstleistung (in der Form von einer passende Gastfamilie/Gastschule) für den SchülerIn erbracht hat.

Positives Feedback: Time of my life, best experience ever, I learned so much, I am so much more independent, I have much more confidence, I am much more aware of my own culture now sind nun einige häufige positive Rückmeldungen die wir immer wieder bekmomen!

Ashley E. Arreola, Eu.MA.sca

into Schüleraustausch GmbH

Währinger Str. 145/15

1180 Wien

fon: +43 1 4787515

YOUR KNOWLEDGE HAS VALUE

- We will publish your bachelor's and
  master's thesis, essays and papers

- Your own eBook and book -
  sold worldwide in all relevant shops

- Earn money with each sale

Upload your text at www.GRIN.com
and publish for free